GOOD USE *of* TIME

GOOD USE *of* TIME

11 Principles to Live By

RAFAEL T. CALDERA

Scepter

Translation of Rafael Tomás Caldera, *El Uso del Tiempo*
(Caracas, Venezuela: Liberil S.R.L. Impresores, 1995).

Copyright © 2013 Scepter Publishers, Inc.
P.O. Box 1391
New Rochelle, NY 10802
www.scepterpublishers.org

Cover and text design by Rose Design

Printed in the United States of America

ISBN: 978-1-59417-185-7

To Don José Agustín Catalá on his
eightieth birthday[1]

---

1. José Agustín Catalá (1915–2011), Venezuelan journalist
and author.

CONTENTS

PROLOGUE

The start of a new year and my recent birthday have stirred up many thoughts and prompted me to write about the fleeting nature of time. Time flows forward inexorably never to return, and one day will bring us all to the shores of eternity.

Everything worthwhile that can be said about time has already been said. St. Augustine in his *Confessions* points to the futility of speaking about time: "What then is time? If no one asks me, I know what it is. If I wish to explain it to him who asks, I do not know."[1] So I don't want to waste any of this treasure, always in such short supply, by adding useless or uninspired words to the wisdom we find in tradition.

---

1. St. Augustine of Hippo, *The Confessions*, ed. Albert Cook Outler (Peabody, Mass.: Hendrickson, 2004), p. 244.

Nevertheless, spurred on by my personal experience of the rapid passage of time, I wish to put into writing some of the traditional counsels that I have found most useful for cultivating the arduous art of making good use of time. I will set down here a brief "compendium" of precepts that I myself want to keep close at hand to inspire me to take better advantage of the days of life that remain to me. For as Pedro Grases[2] warns us so forcefully, we all face the risk of "wasting the definitively non-renewable treasure contained in the useful hours of each day."[3]

My focus here will be squarely and almost exclusively on the good use of time. Little mention will be made of how to better organize our work and carry it out more effectively. Although certainly a useful and practical topic, this would oblige us to enter into an area already covered with great

---

2. Pedro Grases (1909–2004), Venezuelan writer, historian and literary critic. He won the Venezuelan National Prize for Literature in 1993.

3. Pedro Grases, *Obras de Pedro Grases, vol. 19: Un Paso Cada Día* (Barcelona: Editorial Seix Barral, 1993), xvi.

competence by other authors writing for a wide variety of audiences.

"Teach us," the Psalmist asks the Lord, "to number our days, so that we may get a heart of wisdom" (Ps 90:12). Each of our lives is a learning process that can never be repeated. So let us wholeheartedly make the Psalmist's prayer our own.

1.

HE HAS MORE WHO NEEDS LESS

Seeing the time we have at our disposal in life as a fixed amount of capital, the quantity of which is uncertain but never unlimited, can help us to administer it wisely.

So we can begin with a criterion applicable to all material possessions: "He has more who needs less." Perhaps nothing makes us waste time so carelessly (minutes and hours, but also entire days and even years) as the multiplication of unconnected endeavors: the desire to possess, to do, to experience an unending succession of things and situations, which can be summed up in one phrase, the lack of moderation.

When we fail to focus on what is essential in life, our desires and endeavors lose their proper measure. We find ourselves enmeshed in a cloud of evanescent diversions and novelties ever tugging at our hearts.

Haven't we all needlessly multiplied telephone calls, e-mails, meetings? Don't countless books and magazines turn up each day crying out for our attention? Aren't our lives deluged with computers, television programs, films, and music?

Truly, all of us are prone to turning the abundance of opportunities for communication into obstacles to healthy human relationships. I recall a short parable told by a professor of mine about a young fellow eager to see his mother. After fighting the traffic to get to the airport and spending a lot of time waiting for his flight and then in the air, he finally reached his mother's home—only to sit down with her and watch television.

On his ninetieth birthday, the Spanish philologist and historian Ramón Menéndez Pidal evoked the figure of Methuselah. According to legend, this figure from the Hebrew Bible refused to build a house for himself, since he could always find a wall that was already built to provide shelter from the wind and rain. "That's going too far? Without a doubt," Don Ramon admitted. But he also insisted that it is always a good rule to *do without all that we can rightly do without*, so as to make good use of our time. Thus we will never complicate our life with things that, seen properly, have no value or at best are the fruit of disorder and lack of concentration.[1]

Moderation, focusing on what is essential in life, enables our "capital" to yield more. Thus we will live with greater intensity, with self-mastery and a clear focus in all that we do, whether attending to others' needs or simply spending time with them.

So let us be content with our wall, without a roof overhead to protect us.

---

1. See Ramón Menéndez Pidal, "Trabajar Siempre," *El Silencio Creador*, ed. Federico Delclaux (Madrid: Rialp, 1996), pp. 131–132.

2.

TODAY, NOW

The invention of the digital clock, with its precise counting of the minutes and seconds, has awakened in more than one person a vivid awareness of the fleeting nature of life.

Perhaps this is due to its "unidirectional" nature, so different from the cycle of the analog clock, where the hands seem to return to the inconceivable source of an inexhaustible and ever-renewable store of hours, minutes, and seconds. Or perhaps it is because the numerical symbols of the digital clock capture so clearly what is fleeting in a way that not even the steadily falling sand of an hourglass can. Whatever the reason, in the constant pulse of the digital clock we can "see" the rapid passing of time, in all its steady fleetingness.

Contemplating a digital clock and seeing how rapidly the seconds fly by, never to return, we too can be strengthened in our determination not to procrastinate, not to leave things undone for tomorrow, but instead to set to work at what we need to do today and now—*hodie, nunc.*

Everything else being equal, there is a great difference in life between the lives of someone who takes up his tasks right away, applying himself to what he has resolved to do or has the duty to do, and someone who hesitates, a slave to inertia, and habitually postpones what needs to be done until need or the angry demands of others force him to act.

Taking good advantage of time requires being aware of the importance of "today and now." It requires beginning what we need to do, and not putting it off, realizing the value of each moment, even when fatigue or laziness seek to persuade us differently. As Arnold Toynbee once said: "Don't waste odd pieces of time. Don't say to yourself, 'There, I've finished that piece of work, and it's really not worth beginning this next piece till tomorrow morning or till after the weekend. So for the rest of today or the rest of the week I might as well let myself relax and take things easy.' The truth is that you might *not* as well do that; for the right moment for starting on your next job is not tomorrow or next week; it is *instanter*, or, in the American idiom, 'right now.'"[1]

How fruitful time is when we decide to use it well! And how restricted life becomes when one is always waiting for the perfect moment (which of course never comes) to do what needs doing. *Hodie, nunc*: today, now is the right moment to begin.

1. Arnold J. Toynbee, "Why and How I Work," *Saturday Review*, April 5, 1969, p. 27.

3.

URGENT THINGS CAN WAIT

Making good use of time involves, without doubt, knowing how to "squeeze out" each moment in life for all its worth.

When speaking of the end of time, the Gospel delivers a clear judgment on certain especially egregious omissions: the timid and calculating servant who fails to invest the talent he had received and make it earn a return (see Mt 25:14–30); the foolish virgins who didn't take oil for their lamps during their long wait (see Mt 25:1–12); the reprobates who refused to practice works of charity for the most needy (see Mt 25:31–46). Here are parables that mirror our missed opportunities, our wasted time.

Often conspiring against the good use of time is the pressure of "the urgent." This is something that demands to be done with an imperious and immediate claim on our attention: "Right now!" It puts pressure on us, sometimes very forcefully.

But in this very pressure and urgency lie the danger of falling prey to subjectivity in the importance we attach to this pressing demand for action. Often this is easier to see when we ourselves are not the ones feeling the urgency to act but someone else hammering at our door and demanding an immediate response.

Perhaps that is why St. Josemaría Escrivá used to say urgent tasks can wait and the most urgent ones *should* wait. He wasn't recommending delay; he always insisted firmly on the wisdom of the adage "today and now" and the importance of diligent use of time. Rather, he was pointing to the need to distinguish between a task's real importance and its subjective urgency.

Good use of time requires order and setting priorities. We can't do everything at once, but should take up first what is most important. The demand of urgency that attempts to claim for a task an importance it may not really have works against this sound judgment.

Therefore we need to stop and ask: Is this really important? How important? Does it take priority over—have greater importance than—what I was doing or planning to do now?

The key to spending time wisely lies in acquiring the habit of distinguishing between urgency and importance—or, more precisely, discerning the true value and importance of each task, without letting ourselves be dominated by passing emotions. By contrast, in letting ourselves be carried away by what seems urgent, don't we often end up misusing time? And isn't urgency itself often the self-inflicted spur of a lazy person who requires this external pressure in order to overcome himself, shake off passivity, and do what he should?

4.

DEDICATING TIME TO THE GOOD USE OF TIME

Anyone who wants to avoid wasting time throughout the day needs a short plan or program of activities that sets clear priorities and, so to speak, even tries to "foresee the unforeseeable."

This kind of plan doesn't lead to rigidity or tunnel vision. Rather, it helps keep us sensitive to what is truly important each day and may need our immediate attention.

Thus we need to dedicate a bit of time each day to planning our use of time. It should take just a few moments to review the importance each thing really has. With our priorities clearly set, we will be able to tackle each task calmly and energetically.

Since we want to be clear about what is truly important, without falling under the sway of the constant stream of events, we would be wise also to include in our daily plan our fixed obligations: the moments spent around the table after dinner with our family, periods for meditation and prayer, some time each day dedicated to creative work. If our plan includes only each day's passing concerns, these other obligations can easily be slighted, and we can end up doing carelessly what is in fact most important.

Certainly, we will often need to "regroup" and recover our calm amid the clamor of the daily battle. When the telephone rings incessantly, when unexpected visitors turn up, when the clock is ticking relentlessly and the report is due by 5 pm. . . . Then we need to pause for a moment and recover our serenity and a clear vision of why we are working, remembering what our real intention is. Like someone submerged under water, who rises to the surface and gulps air, we can plunge back into what we were doing, with our awareness of why we're doing it refreshed.

"Return, O my soul, to your tranquility,"[1] St. Jerome says with the Psalmist. And he adds: "In every action and in every word may your soul remain composed and tranquil."[2]

---

1. Ps 116:7.

2. See St. Jerome, *Homilies on the Psalms* (*Psalm 116*), trans. Marie Liguori Ewald (Washington, D.C.: The Catholic University of America Press, 2001), p. 289.

5.

PUT YOUR HEART
INTO WHAT YOU ARE
DOING[1]

When we consider each evening how our day has gone, perhaps seeking the unity we sense we have lost, and take inventory of what has been passing through our head, we often find that, to a greater or lesser extent, our actions have been accompanied by a stream of thoughts that pop up without our wanting them and try to prevent us from concentrating on our work. We may find that we have been sidetracked by tasks or concerns we really didn't want to become involved in. As a result, we end the day distracted, unable even to compose our thoughts.

---

1. See St. Josemaría Escrivá's advice in *The Way* (New York: Doubleday, 2006), no. 815.

Often in such circumstances our only recourse will be to trust that sleep will work a miracle, and we will wake up a new person, renewed in body and soul. But sleep by itself is not the remedy. True, the mind carries out a subconscious work of integration while we sleep; but the effectiveness of this work depends on the seeds we have sown while awake.

Distraction generates more distraction. The distracted person's day is frequently a passing from one immediate stimulus to another, some pleasant, others unpleasant, and all of short-term duration. In the end, we find ourselves, as T. S. Eliot said so eloquently, "distracted from distraction by distraction."[2] And in that case who owns our time, our very lives?

Not so with children. Children haven't lost the gift of being completely immersed in what they are doing. Immersed in games that for them are also work, occupations

---

2. T. S. Eliot, "Burnt Norton," first poem of *Four Quartets*, section III, line 12.

that increase their skills and knowledge of the world. For, with Tom Sawyer, children know implicitly that whatever is done with joy is always a game.[3]

Nor have we ourselves forgotten this completely, as from time to time we discover anew when we are fortunate enough to experience moments of intense concentration, when all our faculties are harmoniously integrated in the effort to accomplish the task at hand, with the interior silence that comes with being immersed in a single activity and the absorption that makes us forget the passing of time. Under the spell of such moments, we are like the little girl that Maria Montessori taught,[4] so wrapped up in her play that her teacher was able to raise her from the ground in her little chair without distracting her from what she was doing. At the sight of a child's ability to be

---

3. See Mark Twain, *The Adventures of Tom Sawyer* (Oxford: Oxford University Press, 2007), p. 22.

4. Maria Montessori (1870–1952), Italian physician and educator, founder of the Montessori approach to children's education.

so fully "immersed in the present moment," we adults can only smile.

Certainly, in our case we tend to make everything into work, as Tom Sawyer defined it: anything we are obliged to do without wanting to do it.[5] This very definition, however, gives us the key: to live fully, we must "be in what we do." *Age quod agis*: do what you are doing, putting your whole heart into it. Thus to each task we must give the concentration that only love can give.

This means focusing on what we are doing with the attention of a good artisan, taking meticulous care with each step, each detail in our work. In a word, putting into each task the love that transforms both effort and result into a gift, an offering.

And we need to do this without allowing the next task, perhaps a more attractive one, to distract our gaze from the present moment. St. Thomas Aquinas, who had a proverbial gift of concentration, asked God to grant him the favor of never wanting to

---

5. See *The Adventures of Tom Sawyer*, p. 22.

do things thoughtlessly or getting annoyed at having to do something unpleasant. And he prayed: "O God, grant that I may always restrain my foolish impulses, yet never succumb to lethargy, lest I begin things before I should or abandon them before finishing."[6]

---

6. St. Thomas Aquinas, *Piae Preces*: "Da mihi ut nunquam ea quae fiunt insipienter appetam: et quae fiunt accidiose fastidiam; ne contingat inchoanda ante tempus appetere, aut inchoata ante consummationem deserere." Translated and edited by Robert Anderson and Johann Moser as "To Acquire the Virtues," in *Devoutly I Adore Thee: The Prayers and Hymns of St. Thomas Aquinas* (Manchester: Sophia Institute Press, 2000), p. 39.

6.

FIRST ONE THING, THEN ANOTHER

August 1974, Caracas. The get-together started at the set time and the conversation was flowing smoothly, with questions and answers alternating rapidly despite the visible fatigue—due to illness—of the person at the center of the conversation: St. Josemaría Escrivá. Attending that gathering were many young people, including university and high school students. One of the youngest students raised his hand and asked a question about the good use of time and how to finish things well. If we come to the end of the day with things still left undone, he asked, what should we do?

Given how young the student was, it was hard not to think he was exaggerating a bit. How could this young fellow be so busy?

Nevertheless, St. Josemaría took his question quite seriously (although he couldn't resist adding a small joke), and explained what he himself did in similar situations, giving advice that was useful for everyone.

Many of us present there knew that St. Josemaría's own life was one of constant work ("I'd like to see you in my shoes," he told that young fellow jokingly). We knew he sought to "squeeze out" each moment like a lemon, imparting to it the "vibration of eternity."

In answering the young student's question, he said that anyone with a lot to do usually ends the day with a list of things left undone for the next day. Since we want to make very good use of the time we've been given—never enough for loving and serving, he added—I do first one thing, then another.

This advice, in its very simplicity, is quite demanding: put yourself into the task at hand until finishing it, then move on right away to the next one. Finish each job as well as possible, so that it isn't necessary to go back to it and take time away from other work that's waiting to be done. Overcome laziness, which tries to introduce pauses—each time lengthier—between one task and the next. Eliminate the transitions that, paradoxically, so often impede our going on to the next job. First one thing, then another.

How much time to spend will depend on the particular job. Thomas Edison, it is said, once told a young man who asked for advice on how to work more effectively: "Never look at your watch."[1] Work without concern for the hours and minutes that are passing; don't become distracted by fretting that time is slipping away.

But what should we do if, as often happens, it is hard to find the peace and quiet needed to finish the task at hand, and many other concerns press upon us? Then we can put the alarm on our watch or smart phone to good use. Set the alarm, put it out of sight, and concentrate peacefully on the job

---

1. "Edison" (unsigned article), *La Revue de Shawinigan Falls Review*, May 25, 1932, p. 6.

we want to finish, which becomes our only concern during the time we have allotted for it.

The task at hand then becomes the most important thing we have to do, and we can dedicate ourselves wholeheartedly to it.

7.

MAKE HASTE SLOWLY

The advice comes from antiquity: *festina lente*, make haste slowly, calmly. Or as Pedro Grases, well-known for his capacity for hard work, prefers to translate it: go forward in life *sin prisa pero sin pausa*, "without hurrying, but also without pausing."[1]

The first word, *festina*, brings with it a note of urgency, as though spurring us to overcome any initial passivity and inertia. But the next word, *lente*, presents an apparent contradiction: hurry, but without hurrying.

We shouldn't be surprised by this. What is most important in each person's life can often be captured only in a paradoxical, seemingly contradictory formula. Thus we

---

1. Pedro Grases, *Un Paso Cada Día*, xiii.

attempt to reconcile the deepest realities of human life: self-love and self-giving, freedom and discipline, openness to others and concentration. . . .

Although we will always have to fight against laziness, we must also avoid impetuousness and haste, while striving to preserve the serenity without which any work suffers. As William James said, it is the person who works calmly and without haste, without worrying about the results, whose work is the most productive.

With the sensitivity of an artist working in words, Antonio Machado[2] left us some rich lines that are highly relevant here:

> Slowly and in a clear hand:
> doing things well
> matters more than doing them.[3]

---

2. Antonio Machado (1875–1939), Spanish poet.

3. Antonio Machado, "Proverbios y Cantares," *Poesías Completas* (Madrid: Espasa-Calpe, 1970), 360, no. XXIV: "Despacito y buena letra: // el hacer las cosas bien // importa más que el hacerlas." Translated by Cyril Brian Morris in C. B. Morris, *A Generation of Spanish Poets: 1920–1936* (London: Cambridge University Press, 1971), p. 30.

Slowly: is not an incitement to sluggishness, but a prescription for writing well and clearly. The agitated person falls behind, tries and fails, and has to do things over; he produces unintended results and botches things. "Haste makes waste," as the old saying goes.

True some things have to be done quickly. The surgeon in an emergency room needs to count minutes, perhaps even seconds. Moreover (and leaving aside the fact that the less time one has to do something, the more important it is to be serene so as not to lose even a moment), situations such as these bring into focus an essential element in all our actions, which in other circumstances could go unnoticed: the need for virtue.

Whoever has developed the habit of working well—with the requisite intellectual, moral, and technical virtues—can act surely, quickly, and effectively. The skilled hand moves almost effortlessly, producing the exact right result.

Virtue gives us ownership over our actions. We accomplish what we set out to do, with the greatest economy of effort. Virtue is simultaneously a disposition needed for success in our actions and the perfecting of the person who acts.

This is the point of the second part of Antonio Machado's verse. The external result, brought about by any effective means, is not what matters if the person fails to grow interiorly and loses his vital unity. That would truly be wasting the time which, seen correctly, is our very life.

8.

MANY MEASURES OF OIL CAN BE POURED INTO A BARREL FULL OF NUTS

The wisdom of the Judeo-Christian tradition has passed on to us a saying that can be very helpful when considering how to manage wisely the time we are given as the "capital" of our lives: "Into a barrel full of nuts one can pour many measures of oil."[1]

This image captures quite well what we could call the "elasticity" of time. A barrel seemingly filled to the brim still has room for a lot of oil in the empty spaces between the nuts.

Far from being a rigid framework where nothing more can fit, a day can absorb more

---

1. See Antonin-Gilbert Sertillanges, *The Intellectual Life: Its Spirit, Conditions, Methods*; trans. Mary Ryan (Washington, D.C.: The Catholic University of America Press, 1998), p. 237.

and more items when one strives to fill it to the top. You can have a whole day to write a letter to a family member, yet not find time to finish it. In contrast, when it seems that even a week wouldn't be enough to accomplish what needs doing, you end up surprised that time somehow seems to have slowed down and you've been able to do more than you ever expected. The lazy person ignores this real-life "theory of relativity," which shortens the days of the slothful and lengthens the hours of the diligent.

Here we have a new paradox, verified by experience: only those who are busy have time. On his way to the airport to attend the conclave that would make him pope, Cardinal Wojtyla found time to stop to lend assistance to his parishioners, including an elderly woman who asked him to help look for her lost cat. The miracle is repeated daily: the sun "stands still" for us, as it stood still in the sky for Joshua so that he would have time to defeat the Amorites (see Jos 10:13).

The secret lies in being diligent, in loving, in spending our lives with generosity.

When striving to stretch out our time, however, we need to keep some fixed points of reference in each day, week, and month: activities we should always make time for. Often on the excuse of having a lot to do, we forget that we can end up giving over the better part of our days to sloth. It's not the one who frequently stays late in the office who gets more done, but the one who makes a real effort to get home on time for dinner.

It is only in this tension between the impetus of diligence and the rigidity of the indispensable that we learn to "squeeze out" the juice of time. Only by striving to maintain this balance is our vision sharpened and we find time for everything—as the oil finds room in the barrel between the nuts.

9.

SETTING TIME LIMITS

Another way of gaining ownership over our time is learning to set deadlines.

It's true that our timetable each day already includes time set aside for each activity, with a more or less clearly fixed end point. Many of our endeavors, nevertheless, require more than one day to finish. We may need months and even years to complete them. It is then we run the risk of falling prey to vagueness and never reaching our goal.

To avoid this danger, it can be very useful to estimate the time needed for each undertaking, setting time limits both to the entire project and to each of its stages.

For example, I might tell myself: "This project needs to be finished by next October. To manage that, the first part should be done by May and the second by July. Then I can finish everything by the end of September." In this way, we set certain limits and come face to face, in anticipation, with the fleeting nature of time. Thus we are better able to plan our actions and gain control over what we are trying to accomplish. On reaching a specific date, I can pause and compare what's been done so far with what I had planned, and if necessary adjust the rhythm and intensity of my work.

But won't this careful planning rob my life of flexibility? Won't I become a slave to time? This is a false fear. Setting time limits to accomplish a goal doesn't turn anyone into a slave. A slave is someone who, even as an adult, is dominated by another person's will. Whereas drawing up one's own plan of action is an expression of personal freedom.

Moreover, if at each step we keep in mind the goal we are aiming at and renew our intention to reach it, we give consistency—not rigidity—to our life. Rigidity comes from transforming the means into an end, making the very process of planning into the goal, as if what mattered were following the map rather than reaching the destination.

But when we are determined to attain the goal, especially the final end that is the self-realization of the one who is acting, we will strive to travel toward the goal with a spirit of openness, balancing our plan and its fixed limits with the spontaneity needed to handle whatever might occur.

10.

GROWING ON THE INSIDE

"For everything there is a season," Ecclesiastes tells us, "and a time for every matter under heaven."[1] There are natural rhythms that we observe unconsciously, such as the vital systolic and diastolic rhythms of the heart. Likewise there are rhythms proper to virtue that we need to adhere to, so as not to fail the test of moderation. Lack of moderation ruins everything and can easily lead to the irreparable wasting of time.

We must always remember that there is a season for sowing and a season for reaping; that plants don't grow more rapidly by being tugged at; that knowing how to wait is as important as knowing when to go quickly. Antonio Machado gives poetic expression to this reality in a brief verse:

---

1. Eccl 3:1.

Let things take their time:
for the glass to overflow
you have to fill it first.[2]

Patience is the virtue of those who are convinced that everything doesn't depend on their own efforts—and that their very being has been received as a gift. By patience (which enables us to endure suffering and to learn how to wait, keeping hope alive) we will save our souls.[3]

We need to keep this in mind especially in moments of forced inactivity, when external circumstances place us in a "holding pattern." In *The Way*, St. Josemaria uses farmer's language to remind us that this is the time for "growing on the inside."[4] It is the time for

---

2. Machado, "Proverbios y Cantares," 366, no. LI: "Demos tiempo al tiempo: para que el vaso rebose hay que llenarlo primero."

3. See Lk 21:19.

4. "The plants lay hidden under the snow. And the farmer, the owner of the land, observed with satisfaction: 'Now they are growing on the inside.' I thought of you: of your forced inactivity . . . Tell me: are you too growing 'on the inside'?" St. Josemaría Escrivá, *The Way* (New York: Doubleday, 2006), no. 294.

strengthening the interior life, the relationship with God; it is the time for reflection, refocusing on our daily activities, and rediscovering the value of silence, from which all human words spring. It is the time to redirect the heart toward what is truly important.

Not only will this personal growth lead to greater fruit later on, when circumstances change and we are once again called to immerse ourselves in external activity, but in itself it is time that is redeemed, that is well used.

Learning how to wait and growing on the inside also help us give due importance to resting. Menéndez Pidal, after urging that we devote all our energies to creative work, warns against risking health or equilibrium by "burning the candle at both ends."[5]

We need to learn how to rest, to recover our strength. Sertillanges notes that lack of rest makes us sterile just as much as sloth does. And he warns: "When one does not make room for rest, the rest one does not

---

5. See Menéndez Pidal, "Trabajar Siempre," 134.

take, takes itself: it steals into the work, under the form of distractions, of sleepiness, of necessary things that demand attention, not having been foreseen at the right time."[6] One who fails to make time for resting will have to make time to be sick.

Thus we see clearly how far removed activism is from the good use of time. Running around, hurrying, giving priority to external results, are all marks of our materialistic civilization, which fails to give due importance to the spiritual reality of the human person.

That is why we need the "timeless moments" T. S. Eliot speaks of in his *Four Quartets*. These are moments of contemplation when, absorbed in the present, we leave behind concern for the transient things of this world. Actively inactive, we enjoy in this moment of plenitude a foretaste of eternal life: "Quick now, here, now, always— // Ridiculous the waste sad time // Stretching before and after."[7]

---

6. Sertillanges, *The Intellectual Life*, 245.

7. T. S. Eliot, "Burnt Norton," *Four Quartets*.

11.

REMEMBER THAT ONE DAY YOU TOO ARE GOING TO DIE

To make good use of time, we need to keep in mind its goal. "Remember," counsels Teresa of Avila, "that you have only one soul; that you have only one death to die; that you have only one life, which is short and has to be lived by you alone; and there is only one glory, which is eternal. If you do this, you will stop worrying about many things."[1]

The awareness that life is brief, that it blooms and withers like "a flower of the

---

1. St. Teresa of Avila, "Avisos," *Obras Completas* (Madrid: Biblioteca de Autores Cristianos, 1982), no. 68: "Acuérdate que no tienes más de un alma, ni has de morir más de una vez, ni tienes más de una vida breve y una, que es particular, ni hay más de una gloria, y ésta eterna, y darás de mano a muchas cosas."

field" (Ps 103:15), will help us to concentrate on what is truly essential, seeing each moment as a call from God to live it fully.

Faced with infinite Goodness, the God who truly loves us, and striving to love him in return, we will see all human realities as drawn and guided by that Love. Each of our actions—whether going ahead or waiting, whether engaged in creative work or contemplating created reality—can become an act of love.

And here is the ultimate secret, the key to everything: loving.

Love is the highest and most noble human activity, redeeming every moment we consecrate to it. From love stems diligence, love in action, proper to creatures subject to time, who must strive to act within the constraints imposed by our corporeal condition, with its servitude resulting from sin.

From love, finally, stems patience, which gives us strength against the assaults of time, and enables us to wait—without losing hope—for persons and things to reach their maturity, step by step.

37

Keeping present before us the frontier of death, which lies between time and eternity, will help us to keep on the right course. We will see the briefness of this passing world and grasp its true value as the path to eternal life.

"In the evening of your life, you will be examined on your love,"[2] St. John of the Cross tells us. A love shown in deeds, a patient love. A love that—as the inner source of all our actions—is the core of our personal life. There we find everything.

---

2. St. John of the Cross, "Dichos de Luz y Amor," *Vida y Obras Completas* (Madrid: Biblioteca de Autores Cristianos, 1964), no. 59: "A la tarde te examinarán en el amor."

EPILOGUE

The One who in the beginning created the heavens and the earth, God Almighty, is also the One who brings them to their fulfillment.[1]

For "when the time had fully come, God sent forth his Son, born of woman, born under the law" (Gal 4:4). Through him we have attained freedom from slavery, from sin and death, and with his Spirit we have been given a new life in love.

Wisdom of heart means knowing how to seek, as children, first and in everything the Kingdom of God and his justice. The rest, what we need for our temporal life, will be given to us in addition.

---

1. See Gen 1:1 and *Catechism of the Catholic Church* (Vatican City: Libreria Editrice Vaticana, 1997), no. 302.

"Therefore do not be anxious about tomorrow, for tomorrow will be anxious for itself. Let the day's own trouble be sufficient for the day" (Mt 6: 34).

Here we find a "compendium" of what it means to use time wisely. We are to focus our attention on the present moment, while being concerned above all with its ultimate end, God himself. We are to be immersed in our daily endeavors, without permitting anxiety about the future to creep in, since the future is not in our hands. Trusting in God today, while entrusting to him—truly, with real self-detachment—the future.

For as St. John of the Cross reminds us, "God can only reign in a peaceful and self-detached soul."[2]

Immersed in our daily concerns. With patience. With peace. Letting each day's labor be sufficient for the day, while we await the moment for crossing over the frontier and—on the other side—the definitive arrival

---

2. St. John of the Cross, "Dichos de Luz y Amor," no. 71: "Mira que no reina Dios sino en el alma pacífica y desinteresada."

of the Kingdom, when God will grant us eternal life, "and death shall be no more, and neither shall there be mourning, nor crying, nor pain" (Rev 21:4).